*To the children we used to be,*
*for having the courage to believe in good things*

# Table of Contents

# PREFACE

In May of 1998, my father was in a motor vehicle accident. He was crossing a road and then, like a rag doll, he was thrown up in the air. When he came down, he broke his leg, his arm, his shoulder, all his teeth. For the next three years, he was healing, which translated to a laundry list's worth of medical attention. His leg was amputated. He was diagnosed with throat cancer. He had about 30 intensive surgeries. In the first week of 2001, he went to the hospital for another one of those surgeries. This time it was to address the wiring of his decade old pacemaker, slowly climbing out of his skin. The morning before his surgery, he had a cardiac arrest (a phrase I used to pronounce as cardia-caress). He fell into a coma, which had happened before. But this time it was longer. He was comatose for three months. And then he died. I was eight. My brother was six. My mother was devastated.

This year marks the 15th anniversary of my father's death. I am 23 years old. All my big, life-altering moments have happened without my father, but so have my quiet, slow-changing moments. My father has been absent from my everything: my graduations, my love stories, my inconsequential failures. When I think about the person I am becoming, I always wonder if my father would recognize me. More importantly, I wonder if he would like me.

*When I'm Not There* is a collection that I wish existed when I was eight years old and I had no idea how to handle my overwhelming grief. I wish it existed when I was 18 and my grief had become as comfortable as my favorite pair of jeans. I even wish I had this to read now, when it seems like I am racing towards a future my father could never have predicted. I needed this book so badly, that I knew that I had to be the one to write it.

This book is fiction the way our dreams are fiction. Initially, I was embarrassed to share this project, to even discuss it with family and friends: imagine, a series of poems written by a daughter in her dead father's voice to that same daughter. The hardest part about writing these poems was admitting one of my biggest, most private secrets to the rest of the world. For me, my father has not been absent. He has been witnessing my life's unfolding. He has been there for me in a way that no living parent could possibly be. I have thanked my father for all my triumphs and cursed at him in my moments of desperation. I have carried his memory with me to every city, every country, every continent I have ever visited. I have been imagining my father's voice, his attitudes and beliefs for so long, that it was remarkably easy to write some of these poems. I know what he would think of my boyfriend, of my skewed sleeping patterns, of my even temper. I know how he would feel as easily as I know how I would feel.

But I wanted to do this right. I wanted these poems to be authentic not only to my father's memory, but also to the person he really was. I dug through his old notebooks, his manuscripts. In the months leading up to his death, he drafted a dark-humored book about his experience as a patient with multiple illnesses. He titled it *How To Make Millions Without Killing Your Patients*. The acknowledgment for that work is on the following page. It is proof of his creativity and his optimism. My father thought he would survive. I thought he would survive.

Writing these poems in my father's voice meant that I could not use my own. This is the only time you will hear from me in this entire volume – at least if you pretend, at least if you believe that there is something else out there. That my father really has been at the edge of the universe, peering down at my life.

In that case, I want to say something only I can say: the grief I have shouldered for my father has never once felt like a burden. Where I come from, grief is another side of love. I love my father. I miss him in a way that would astonish my younger self, who would never have understood this kind of commitment. Fifteen years ago, when my father died, all I wanted was for time to crawl back. Now, I am all grown up and time isn't crawling at all. It is zooming ahead. My father used to lift me on his shoulders. Now, I'm the one carrying him.

# ACKNOWLEDGEMENT

*While I clung to every thread of life in the ICU, it was my wife who prayed and held my hand. My family needed a lot more than life – they were asking for a miracle. Whether it was luck. God. Faith. Or true love, I will never know. But whatever it was, it worked. And, I'm alive today to write this book.*

*I thank the brilliant Surgeons, Doctors and Medical team who never gave up on me. Even up to the last minute they demonstrated faith like it has never been defined before. This book is my way of appreciating you. Remember you encouraged me!*

*I also want to thank my children, Yena, my daughter and Amit, my son who in their own way asked God to spare my life.*

*Once again, Meena, if words could say it, it's not in the Dictionary*

*Yena and Amit for those tiny hands that rubbed my back when I was in pain,*
*Thank You.*

– excerpt from Vivek Sharma Purmasir's manuscript,
*How To Make Millions Without Killing Your Patients*, 2000

# Your Lullaby

*Zaval, Zaval goes to school*

*Zaval, Zaval is a very good girl*

*Zaval, Zaval has a lot of friends*

*Zaval, Zaval makes Mommy and Daddy very proud*

*Zaval, Zaval will meet a very nice boy*

*Zaval, Zaval will get married and come live at home*
*and the boy will live down the hall*

*Zaval, Zaval is everyone's favorite girl*

*Zaval, Zaval is very, very happy*

*Zaval, Zaval is getting quiet*

*Zaval, Zaval is falling asleep*


*Zaval, Zaval can sing this song all by herself*

# After I Died

You were the last person who believed I was still alive.

On the night that I died, you were sleeping,
unconscious and slowly breathing.
I like to imagine that for one final moment,
we were in the same space.

This is only a miracle because of the way that you tell it.

This is only a miracle because you were my baby girl
and suddenly you were vicious and inconsolable.

As you got older, this was how you would act
in the face of grief: tough and crazy and stupid.

My stupid baby. My sleeping baby.

You were the last person who believed I was still alive.
On the night that I died, you still hoped
and wished and yearned. You, crying and shaking,
you, snapping and yelling,

> *YOU'RE MAKING THIS UP*
> *THIS CAN'T BE TRUE*
> *THIS CAN'T BE REAL*

Oh honey, it is

and it isn't.

# Your First Funeral

So you want to know, what happened after I died?
I'll tell you.

The nurses cleaned my body and put me in a white tracksuit.
One of them brushed my hair. I was carried, like a baby,
to a place no one ever wants a baby to go to.

But Amit and you were peering down
at my dead old man face. Your Mommy was gripping
the red wood coffin. This wasn't the funeral yet
and we were still alone.

What's the difference between a dead man and a coma man?
Nothing, really.

Nothing, until the funeral.

You know, I think it's gross and unfair
that we had an entire day to say goodbye
and I couldn't speak.

You and Amit, too young to speak.
Your Mommy, too sad to speak.

Anyway, it was mostly boring. You had that teddy bear
that I didn't give you. Your brother clutched
stems of flowers. Your mother wore a white sari.
I had never seen your mother wear a white sari.

And then it wasn't boring anymore. Then my babies
touched my feet and my sweetheart
was sobbing. If I wasn't dead already,

this monumental moment would have killed me.

But I was dead, I was dead and you were watching my body
fold into an oven, bigger and more permanent
than any fairytale.

Hey, here is a fairytale:
Daddy died and you live happily ever after.

When you got older, you said that if I wasn't dead before,
I was definitely dead after the cremation,
which sounds like all the hurt and sarcasm of my old heart.
Because, of course, what is there after a cremation?

Just some smoke, some dust.

You.

Another memory of us.

# Trading Worlds

Where I came from, terrorism
was just another word for home.
I grew up knowing how to be scared and wanting to fight.

That was in South Africa and in India,
your mom grew up knowing the same things.

Do you know what people thought of America? Safety.
White men and black men and brown men. Living
and working.

Do you know what people thought of South Africa? Chaos.
White men and black men and brown men.
Not knowing who to look at on a street,
not knowing where to walk on a street.

But my children weren't supposed to flinch, weren't supposed
to watch the news with open mouths, weren't supposed
to have nightmares that looked like headlines.
Ask your mother, ask her.

She'll tell you how they put up black screens
on window panes,

how we would've done anything to stay alive,
even if it meant pretending not to be alive.

Would we have come here if it was going to be
exactly the same?

I wasn't alive the day the Twin Towers came down,
but it didn't matter that I had been dead for six months.
My wife and children on opposite sides of a city,
me forever faraway. When your teacher asked
if everyone was okay,
I know you wanted to say no.

You talked to a boy at school, his father was a firefighter,
he died in one of the towers. You were nine years old,
offering to shoulder a stranger's grief like you weren't scared
of pain,

like you were growing from it,
like you were learning to love it.

# Crushed

When you're young and life doesn't go according to plan,
someone will inevitably say that things will get better
when you're older.

I know, because that's what I want to say.

Wait until you're older. I can't give you any more advice,
can't say I'm happy about you needing a lucky pink shirt,
staring at the mirror, and sucking in your belly.

This isn't love yet, honey, not even close,
but you don't want to hear that. What's worse is
that you don't want to believe that. You think
love is all crying and puking, all writing his name
in the margins of your notebook.

You want a story? Imagine me, 11 years old and wanting
to feel real. Imagine some girl with an easy smile.
Sounds good, but it didn't work out

and now, now it's easy to see why.

When you look back on your life, things will make sense
and you will forget what it felt like to want someone so badly,
you would have eaten paper if he dared you to.
You would have told him your truth if he asked you to.

It won't be like this again. You're going to grow up
and meet someone who will look at you
like all the lights are finally turning on.

Honey, all the lights are finally turning on.

Get up.

It's time for school.

# Valentine's Day

What kind of child does something equal parts thoughtful
and equal parts morbid? That Valentine's Day card
you wrote for your mom, how you signed my name on it.

That's a scary gesture, honey.
You can't just will love into existence,

but you're right, you can't quite ignore it either.

Of course, love doesn't die, but it has to get quiet.
It takes another form and anyway, you ask your mother
if she's happy and she'll tell you she's happy,

but love isn't just about being happy.

Love is putting a twin bed next to a full bed,
love is a blue nightgown and a pharmacy on speed-dial.

You wrote down a message and signed my name,
promising that I would love your mother forever.

Which is the truth, which is worth stating
and restating.

Did I tell you about the day we met? On the list
of things I should have told, this sits at the top.

God, are you old enough for this story yet?
Have you found my old journal yet? I loved your mother
with all the courage and audacity

9

I could have mustered. It did not feel like enough.

She loved me the way people hope to be loved,
with humility and dignity and unwavering faith.
Like I was a prayer and she wanted to worship.
Like I was sick and she wanted to heal.

Oh baby, are you gonna love someone like that some day?
What a lucky someone.

# Hindsight

So Amit got glasses, which means
we could have been the kind of four-eyed family
that relieved bookish kids everywhere.

But you're not wearing your glasses anyway,
squinting at the blackboard and blinking
at the television screen. My almost perfect girl,
seeing only what you want to see.

Do you really think Amit will grow up to look
like me? One day, when he's older, smoking,
graying hair?

You're the one trying on my old glasses, wearing
my pajamas to bed. When you're hunched over
your computer keyboard, it almost looks like
I'm still alive.

I have this theory, that Amit isn't going to look
like me forever. One day, he'll grow into
your mother's face. One day, his eyes
will be just like her eyes.

But you, with hands that look like my hands,
and you're typing so much faster.

# Forgiving God

Maybe I'm the lucky one,
because I never got to experience
the brunt of your disappointment, your anger.
Boy, can you hold a grudge.

When I was a kid, my oldest sister left home
in such a huff. She would come visit,
but she never really came back.

You have been telling anyone willing to listen
that you don't believe in God. If someone asks why,
you say it's because you're mad at Him.

*How can you be mad at God,* they ask.
You tell them, *My father is dead.*

If I believed in God, I think I could forgive Him.
But you didn't just believe in God. Baby, you thought
you really knew Him. Like a friend,
like a promise.

Do you think you'll ever be able to sit in temple
and not think about this tremendous let-down?
Apparently, you can beg for something and still
not get it.

Hey, even if you don't go back, you should at least go visit.

Anyway, of course you still believe in Him.
How else could you possibly believe in me?

# What the Dead Need

This only works because of the way you picture me.
Right now, you haven't decided if I'm in heaven, or
somewhere in-between. When I'm not there with you,
it's because I'm at the edge of the universe, peering down.

You sometimes imagine that I'm eating breakfast
with my parents, my brother,
people I never thought I would get to see again.

But sometimes, you give me nothing.
I've got all the space and all the time,
but I've got it all alone.

Which is okay too. I understand. When I'm not there,
you forget I was ever a real person. And it's hard
to remember what a person needs.

Especially a dead person.

## Playing Pilot

When I was alive, I used to travel. When I died, Amit
used to tell his friends that I was a pilot. It's a joke because
you don't know where I am, just that I'm not coming back.

The first time you visited a country I had never seen
it was New Zealand. You stayed at my sister's house
and looked out her windows at the widening clouds.

That sky looked nothing like my old sky, but at least
you were in the Southern Hemisphere and at least
that was something. For one whole summer,
you heard lilting South African accents.
Accents like my accent, just in a different place.

On a map, all anyone can see is the stretching distance.
Is there a map between reality and impossibility?
If I really was a pilot, I'd want you to build my itinerary.
If I really was a pilot, I'd go where you go.

# Blooming

## I.

When I was 12, a girl had a stack of sanitary napkins
peeking out of her backpack and like any blooming asshole,
I took one out of its wrapping and stuck it on the back
of her uniform blouse. It was just an idea and then suddenly,
it was more than an idea. It was real. It's worth remembering
that she liked me. When I think of this story,
I always remember that she really liked me. Me,
the epitome of cool and cruel. For the rest of the day, she sat
in class, looking like a joke. Of course, everyone noticed.
They all laughed. I just grinned, like I was so proud of myself.

## II.

When you were 12, you stayed after school at a reading club,
sitting at a desk and deeply examining obscure character
development. When you tried to stand up,
you felt the familiar peeling of wet denim. No surprise when
you saw the puddle of blood, bigger than the size of your
head. *I'm going to die*, you thought, but you meant
out of embarrassment. How'd you clean everything
up before your 80 year old teacher noticed? Some soap and
paper towels, I guess. The epitome of nervous and cool,
you tied your jacket around your waist and then hailed a bus.
At home, you stood in the bathroom and rinsed
out your jeans for ten minutes, until all the blood washed out.
The next time you wore them, no one else noticed a thing
and you were so proud of yourself, you couldn't stop smiling.

# No Stone Tower

It's easier to think that this is all my fault, my absence.
That this never would have happened if I was still alive.
But the truth is that even if I was there,
I couldn't protect you from a day like today.

Even if I locked you in a stone tower, honey,
I couldn't keep you safe.

Do you remember when that man tricked you
into drinking the vodka? You were six.
I was living and livid.

You looked like a woman betrayed. You were six
and you looked like a woman betrayed. I know,
I've seen that look, from my mother, my sisters,
your mother, her sisters. Women grow to own that look:
my daughter, sitting in a train car, horrified and nauseous.
How you rode the rest of the way with wide eyes,
glancing over your shoulder at the subway poles.

And then you went shopping. And then you bought your
dress, all pink and cream.
And then you went to the dance, looking like a princess.

Just a princess. No stone tower.
No magic curse.

If I wrote this story, it would be exactly like this
and you wouldn't need to be saved from anything.

# An Almost Accident

I know what a car wreck looks like,
honey, and you aren't one. But you're on a bus
and you're thinking you're lonely.
You're thinking life is a swamp and you're sinking.

No, your friends don't get it
and your family doesn't want to get it.

You used to smile so much,
and now, you don't.

You think of me fondly and then bitterly.

Did I ruin your life?

I don't know a girl brave enough
to pray for her father's soul and then go to a concert.
I don't know you, honey,

but you know me. You know I love you and I'm sorry.
You know it's cold outside and you're hungry.
You keep turning your phone off and on, because
you know a bad idea when you have one.

Honey, this is a bad idea.
Get off the bus.
Call a friend.

I know what an accident looks like,
and it's always just a small thing.

Honey, you aren't a small thing, but you're no giant either. If you run away, it will take more than some magic beans to find you.

Do you know what I miss the most about my life? Home.

# History of Heart Disease

I.

You broke your hand when you were six years old
and we used to scratch underneath our casts together.
I showed you how to use a pencil, but you still tried to
wedge your pinky finger underneath all that plaster. I never
thought we would share another physiological failure.
But now you're wearing a heart monitor, a metal box
taped to your sternum, so that the doctor can check
if you're living right by a series of zig zag patterns
on a piece of paper. That sounds like art, right, and you're
going to use this for art, right. You're fifteen, right,
and nothing bad is going to happen to you. Right.
Right.


II.

Here is what dying feels like: like the world shuttering
to a close. Here is what living feels like: like blinking
at the face of someone shaking your shoulders.
*Hey, hey, you're okay* he says and you sit up and smile
that winning cover girl smile. But the paramedic won't have
it. And the nurse at your fancy college won't have it. And
your mother on the phone when you tell her, is angry
and scared. So, you come home and meet with five
doctors who run complicated tests and tell you a series
of the same thing, the thing you have heard your entire life:
*You have to learn to live with this.* And you're better than me,
because you will.

# Dream Deferred

You got a tiny college letter and you can sum it up
in an even smaller word. Deferred doesn't mean rejected,
baby. It just means that you need to wait. But
you hate waiting, have been waiting your whole life
for things to change. It sounds fake when anyone tells you
now that it will get better. No, not from your experience.
In your experience, things slow down and then
they get worse. Okay, baby, if it makes you feel better,
you can imagine your worst case scenario.
You can imagine a monster but that doesn't make it real.
I know your reality, which is that your life will be full of
laughter and books and lush hills. Remember when you were
five years old? We went to the zoo. We had to wait
for the bus. You were impatient and excited.
But the bus came, right? We saw the lions and peacocks.
You rode on a camel. Do you remember waiting for the bus?
No, probably not. I can't think of a reason why you would.

# Stage Whispering a Milestone

The day you found out that you got into your dream school,
it was also my death anniversary.
But you were laughing and dancing,
clutching a piece of paper so tightly it almost crinkled,
but my girl, smoothed it out.

My girl can smooth anything out,
even pain. God, it should have always
been like this. And maybe, it always was
like this. You used to take you first grade spelling tests
with all the seriousness of a respected scholar.

The way you celebrated, it felt like you were
still a child, sitting at the foot of your mother's bed
and chattering away:

> *Daddy died years ago today,* you said,
> *but it doesn't feel that way. It feels like he's here.*
> *It feels like I'm supposed to be happy.*

You have loved the sound of other people telling you
that I would've been proud of you. It has always been true,
but on this day, it was like fire. On this day, it was me
stage whispering:

> *my baby who used to read picture books with me*
> *and tried to memorize the multiplication table*
> *before she was in kindergarten, my baby got into college*
> *i am so proud of you, so incredibly proud*
> *just this once, i wish i could tell you myself.*

# And Thereafter

You got your practice praying for my life
when I was still alive, but you became an expert
after I died. Through elementary and middle school,
you used to secretly pretend that the right combination of
words and songs would change things back.

Honey, things don't change back. And it's crazy
to want them to.

You kept praying for a dead man to come back to life,
like it was a game. And it was a game
until you had the nightmare that I died again.
That wasn't a nightmare, baby. It was a promise.

Don't you know by now, that no one lasts forever?
Even you are different now, older and less focused on magic.

Sometimes, you have that dream that you bump into me
on the street. I look at you like I don't know you
and you wake up crying. When you were a girl,
you would've thought that was really me.

But you're not a girl anymore and I'm not your friendly ghost.

I'll be dead for the rest of your life and all the lives thereafter.
What you miss about me, you're going to have to find in
someone else.

# Blessing

The day you packed your bags for college, the family priest
was loading everything into his car. When you were
a little girl, this was the man you hated. It was easy enough,
because he scolded you when you got the havan samagri
on his carpet. And you had never been scolded before.

But if there was anyone who could get someone to love them
with minimal effort, it had to be you. Now, the priest
thinks of you like his own daughter. And you're so grown up,
you don't even spill the samagri on his carpet anymore.
He's blessing you, seeing in your face all the things
I had always seen.

# Age of Aquarius

When I was alive, you had a handful of friends
we'd invite for birthday parties, but no real best friend.
The kids who lived next door were like cursory cousins,
promising to come over and then hours later,
you'd realize that they wouldn't. I told you then,

that I'd be your best friend, but you hated that.
*Daddies aren't best friends*, you said, *they're family.*
That's true, but, anyway, it was nice to pretend. I made
you laugh and we played games until it was dinner time.

It was a year after I died that you met Vivian. The moment
you became best friends was the moment you told her
about me, which was also the moment she told you
about her parents' divorce.

Which was also the moment when you both first talked.

But after that, it was impossible not to talk,
not to share the hard, similar family stories
of lonely mothers and angry younger brothers. Just two girls
laughing on the phone, or typing away on the computer.

No matter what anyone tells you, it's a special thing
to be loved. When someone can giggle at your jokes
and still have the sensitivity
to read your dead father's old journals.

What I'm saying is, it's not always so different.
If you're lucky, your best friend becomes your family.

# The Love Poem

Do dead people have any kind of clairvoyance? Can we see
things for what they are? When you fell in love
for the first time, I had this thought. That I wanted
the divine power to see how it would unfold. That sounds
like morbid fascination. It wasn't. It was your scared,
nervous father. It was the way you used to sit alone in your
college dorm, whispering to your friends that something
was wrong. No one ever believes a pretty girl when she says
something is wrong. But something was wrong because you
loved a boy and you were keeping it a secret. It just didn't
seem right. My girl who laughed loudly and cried hardly.
What were you doing, loving quietly?

# Some Other Life

When the first man you loved betrayed you, there was no
*I told you so*, no smug shrug at the dinner table. Anyway, he
was a fucking asshole and if I had the talent,
I'd haunt the shit out of him. But that's a lie.

If I had the talent, I'd sit at the foot of your bed
and joke about his eyebrows, his pathetic music collection.
Anything to make you smile, or eat a meal, or meet
someone else again. No, that's a lie,

because I am worried about the world and you in it.
And if I had the talent, I'd carry you over on a hot air balloon
and you'd look down from the sky. And up there,
you'd tell me

that you loved someone and he hurt you.

And I would have nothing to say, nothing to offer
but my anger and hatred for a boy, that in some other life,
could have been my friend. In some other life, you
would have been a girl

in a window, looking down and frowning.
And if you had told us then that he hurt you,
we would have laughed. Do you know the sound
of boys laughing? What am I saying? Of course you do.

# Warming & Warning

You were going to a party, so you bought
a sheer lace woven top, the hemline barely
skimming your waist. You tried it on at home
and then stood in the kitchen, laughing.
Amit opened his mouth, and you raised your eyebrows.
This is the kind of thing we both would have
struggled with. You, half-naked
and posing for a photo with your friends.
A boy from your college, twice your size
and four times your strength, told you
that he was afraid of you, how easily
you could cut him down. Like a dying tree.
You are not a dying anything. What I would've
thought about your clothes and your choices
wouldn't have changed a thing in your mind.
But you would've changed mine. My beautiful
daughter in a slinky black dress and then
crawling into a pair of fleece pajamas.
The way the sun looks when it's blazing at noon
and later when it's tucking itself in at night.
Still the same sun. Still the same girl, warming
and warning. Even if I could have said something
about your short shorts, I still would've been silent.
I would've taken one look at your eyebrows
and known to shut the fuck up.

## Slow Burning

If you douse an entire house with gasoline, it's always
vulnerable to a flicker, even a virgin matchstick poses a threat.

You are not that house, but you are the daughter
of a man who used to keep a handle of vodka
on the top of the refrigerator.

Doesn't matter that you didn't start drinking
until you were legal, it matters how you're drinking.
Sometimes just at a party, and sometimes shots in the
morning. Sure, someone just broke your heart,
but it's the way your brain works that scares me.

I knew a brain like that.

Don't you remember when you ate my birthday cake
and I threw the leftover slice against the kitchen walls?
It made a mess and there were crumbs everywhere.

This is a gross story and I know you think so.
I know because I saw your face, saw how you
flinched when I drank the beer
that looked like apple juice, but was never just apple juice.

The world today isn't that different. People are still the same,
transfixed when a skinny alcoholic
stands up straight,
like it's a magic trick.

But it doesn't make pain disappear.

Everything becomes sticky, your table tops
and your thoughts:

what a stupid metaphor, why would anyone want to
douse a house with gasoline?

# In the Amphitheater

The President was a woman in black robes and the faculty
were in black robes and somewhere in a crowd
of young people, my daughter in a black robe.
And the President said:

*you should all stand up and turn around and thank your parents.*

So, you stood up and you knew where your mother was,
the way all children can pinpoint on a map the exact location
of their mother, can even tell you the latitude longitude
of their birth, from pure memory.

So, you started crying because your mother was standing
and waving. Your mother has always been standing
and waving. Anyway, this is probably a tradition at
graduations, but what do I know?

The last graduation I was at was my own.

No, my children never looked back at me,
never felt my stare as they clutched a fake diploma.

It's like I wasn't there, which of course,
I wasn't.

The President asked the graduating class to clap
for their families, everyone who supported
the academic rat race, who answered late night phone calls
and mailed care packages, who had to tolerate

holidays and weekends of all-nighters.
Your mother who read all your papers
and could talk to you about them.

So you clapped your hands for her. And then,
when you sat down and faced that stage again,
you clasped your hands for me.

# The Grace of Giving

As a child, you used to wear your hair in two thick braids
so often, that your hair used to bend and curl.
I told you once, that if you weren't good, I'd chop it all off.

But you were always sweet, smiling even when
you were crying. Of course, your hair grew three feet long,
waving at the ends, almost like it was
saying goodbye.

My beatific girl. When the time came, you cut your own hair,
held the scissor in your hands while your mother took
a picture. Ten inches and you put it in a ziplock bag,
ready to mail. Ready for someone else to use.

Your hair skimmed inches past your shoulders,
pin straight, so different from how it looked before
and just as lovely.

You have done the kindest things in my name.
Imagine someone wearing a wig made of the hair
I used to brush. Those black ends waving,
saying hello, promising a legacy of something good.

# Keeping Company

Before I was sick, we used to have people over all the time,
parties every month and dinners in-between.

So, no, I never knew what it was like to be alone.

When I was at the hospital, I'd call home every night
and on the weekends, you'd all come visit. I like to think
that there was a great lesson in that, that you learned
exactly what to do when you were away at college.

So, when you had a frustrating discussion section, or
needed to vent about your thesis, your mother would hum
into your ear. And on her birthday or Diwali,
you'd come home.

When she and Amit would visit you, they'd bring boxes
of home-cooked food, for you and your friends.
After four years away on some countryside,
your mother had effectively adopted twelve other girls.

What should have been the loneliest time for all of you
turned out to be just fine. And now, there's a steady stream
of visitors sleeping on the couch.

When someone loves you, they ache to see you.
When you love someone, just laughing together
feels like a party.

# One Day a Relic

You applied to twelve graduate schools and got rejected
from every single one. My girl who used to dream
of long hallways and a heavy briefcase, like my briefcase,
has to pack a purse for the office,
has to tell the world that something
isn't happening. The whole world thought it was happening,

but you come live at home and rest your feet
on your mother's bed. You don't talk to me
as much as you used to, but when you do, you're crying and
telling me that you failed. You say that word like it's a curse,
like it physically hurts you,

like you never failed before,

which means your dad has a shadow you wouldn't recognize,
wouldn't understand. Go into the kitchen and open
that cupboard, the one with all the mugs
from the BABY YENA company.

Honey, that's a failure, but it had your name on it and I got
to see your face light up every time we talked about
my ambitions that didn't add up.

You think you failed, so you want to burn all your notebooks.
But imagine if you named your biggest failure
after someone you loved. You still wouldn't want it,
but you'd have to keep its extra pieces in drawers and folders.

This time, that you hate, that is just waiting for the next
adventure, is the time that someone else cherishes.
When you're gone, across the country or the river,
someone else will open up the cupboards, and look
at your pathetic first drafts.

What I mean is, when someone loves you,
they are proud of your everything.

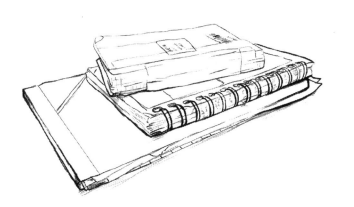

# Sand Storm

The third time you went to New Zealand, you went because
you wanted to shake love out of yourself, like you could
pour sand out of a bottle without making a mess.

But you had to collect the sand first,

so you trekked to different continents and kept your mother
on speed-dial. You talked about me to people in cities
I had only heard of in books and movies. Now,
those strangers know our family saga. When they think
of America, they can think of our pain.

In India, you clipped my oldest sister's toenails humbly,
saying that I wouldn't have had it any other way.
That's a sweet sentence, if it were true.

In New Zealand, you helped another sister move
her plateware. She was old and couldn't bend her knees.
She looked at a sturdy tray, saying she would give it to you
as a wedding present. *Move here,*
she said. *We'll find you a good Kiwi boy.*

The third time you went to New Zealand, your mother
had a nightmare that you didn't come back
and then you called, because you fell on your back
in the middle of the street, and thought of me,
on my back, in the middle of another street.

When you were down there, you thought you could stay there
forever. You had breakfast with a man you loved.

He loved you too, but you didn't really believe it until
you were packing a bag for California.

You went to California because your best friend from college
was there. Another one of my sisters is also there,
but you didn't see her. That's a tragedy because, well,
she loved me the most. Now, your friend moved back home.
I guess, everything happens the way you want it to.

Just when I start to think you're nothing like me, you go
and do something exactly like me. Just look at this mess.
Look how we're trying to clean it up.

## *How To Make Millions Without Killing Your Patients*

was a title that people would remember, but you named
your books with the simplest language, the words people
use everyday and just as easily forget. I think that's a dirty
trick. I think it's clever shit. I think that you're writing
the way I used to write. But the clock you're racing against,
it's all pride. Me, I was racing against my life.

What sustains a person is the lie, that the things we dream up
hold value and purpose for someone else.
You and I, with notebooks and lists and doodles
arrogant enough to be called art. Do you really believe
your pithy experiences would matter to someone else?

You really do, don't you? If anyone can understand that,
it's me. You found my manuscript and saw
the nitty gritty potential of a fumbling artist. You showed it
to your best friend and she said *He is a good writer.*
She knows I'm dead, but for a moment, it didn't matter.
For a moment, I was alive again.

# Waves of Harmony

When the boy you're dating finally came home,
you both sunk into the cushions of the daybed.
My garlanded picture hung over your young,
tender heads. If something bad was going to happen,
the frame would have dropped, would've given
him a well-deserved concussion.

But nothing bad was going to happen.

After all, he drank your mother's tea and laughed
at your brother's jokes. If I was there, I would've
given him a no-nonsense handshake.
Then, I would've asked him to sing. You like to think
you'd object, laugh that precious embarrassed laugh.
But, baby, you wouldn't have. You would have listened.
What the hell, you would have joined him.

## Reply to Sender:

When I first died, you used to write me letters,
come home and then read them aloud.
Now, you don't do that. You don't write me
and you don't talk to me. Where is the girl
who used to push all her thoughts
out to the universe, thinking by a miracle
it would reach me? She's growing up
and talking about me without flinching,
without crying. Now I'm not a deep secret.
Just a sad fact that you can pull out when
it's easy. This is just the beginning of fading
into obscurity and I wish it would end here,
but you've got your whole life ahead
and I'm the one already looking back.
Remember when you used to fight anyone
who told you it was time to let go? Now what?
Now you don't miss me? Okay, forget everyone
else. At least fight with me.

# Traditions of Mourning

Now that you're all grown up, I imagine
what you must look like:
like my mother, maybe,
with her long black braid, her perfectly pleated sari,

her yellow-sick skin.

The shadow memory of a woman I barely got to know.
Just like you.

I am just like you.

# When I Think About Your Future

In my head, you get married.
In my head, you get married and your husband
loves you so much, he cries just thinking about it.

In my head, you have children
that have your dimple-smile mouth. You help
them with their homework and projects
and they do so well, everyone thinks they cheated.

You live in a house in Connecticut. You eat sausages
and pancakes on the weekends.

Unless you're a lawyer, you don't think about lawyers.

Unless you're a doctor, you don't meet doctors.

You don't cry about me anymore. You certainly
don't cry about anything else.

No, that sounds good, but it's a lie. I hope,
no matter how perfect your life is, no matter
how fulfilled and happy you become,
that you still cry about me from time to time.
I hope you remember.

Even if it's just on March 28th. Even if it's just because
you loved me once. How can you forget someone
you loved once? I can't.

No matter how big you get.
No matter how long it's been.

There is no time for me. Every single moment
of your future has felt the same.

# Voiceless

When I was diagnosed with throat cancer, we made
plans to record my voice. Do you remember?

Your mom and I, we said we wanted you and your brother
to remember what I sounded like. We thought
there would be a time, when I would sit with you, silent.

Even then, I wanted you to remember the way I laughed.

We bought tapes. We had a machine.
There was a schedule. Even a script.

But we never recorded my voice. I died
before that. There's one video tape of me,
which is something you can watch and rewatch.

But it's not me laughing. It's not me saying your name.

I loved your name. I named a company after your name.
If I could, I would've named the world after your name.

What does Yena mean? One who prays.

Isn't that something? You were praying for me
at the end, but you were also praying for me
from the very beginning.

Even your first word was *Da-da*.

Maybe it's a blessing that there are no tapes, that there's no way to pretend I'm still talking.

It wouldn't have been enough. I don't know how I could even begin to thank you.

# About the Author

Yena Sharma Purmasir is a poet from New York City. She was the Queens Teen Poet Laureate for the 2010-2011 academic year. Her first book of poetry, *Until I Learned What It Meant*, was published by Where Are You Press in 2013. Purmasir graduated from Swarthmore College in 2014 with a major in Psychology and a double minor in English Literature and Religion Studies. She was the recipient of the Chuck James Literary Prize from Swarthmore College's Black Cultural Center. She served in the New York City Civic Corps program, dedicating 10 months of service at Hour Children, a non-profit supporting formerly incarcerated mothers and their families. Purmasir currently works at the Louis August Jonas Foundation, helping organize and implement their international scholarship program, Camp Rising Sun. She believes in the power of hard work, second chances, and, above all, love.

To read more of her work, visit:
**fly-underground.tumblr.com**

Made in the USA
Middletown, DE
13 March 2019

# DARK RITES